Downshifter's
Cartoon B

Les Ellis

ISBN 978-1-904871-83-5
A catalogue record for this book is available from the British Library.

Published by
The Good Life Press Ltd.,
The Old Pigsties, Clifton Fields,
Lytham Road, Preston, PR4 OXG
www.goodlifepress.co.uk
www.homefarmer.co.uk

THIS YEAR HE RESOLVED TO GET BACK TO NATURE....
WHAT BOTHERS ME IS THE DOWNSIZING!

Les does

A Pen of Pigs
Down the Allotment
Foodie Matters
All Sorts of Eco Stuff
A Field of Cows
Wildlife
You're Not from Round Here, Are You?
Red Tape
Sheep Hurdles
Poultry Matters

A Pen of Pigs

SO HE'S GOT ME ON 60 A DAY...APPARENTLY THE FLAVOUR'S MUCH BETTER AFTER SMOKING.

Down the Allotment

MIKE MADE A MENTAL NOTE NOT TO MAKE HIS OWN NETTLE FERTILIZER AGAIN.

POOR ROSE, SHE WERE ME FAVOURITE COLLIE.

COMPANION PLANTING No 9... THE DOG ROSE

BEEKEEPING IS SO WORTHWHILE. SHE USED TO SPEND A FORTUNE ON BOTOX.

COURGETTES, I'VE HAD A FEW, BUT THEN AGAIN, TOO FEW TO MENTION.

FRANK HAD A POOR CROP. HE HAD IGNORED THE ADVICE AND DID IT HIS WAY....

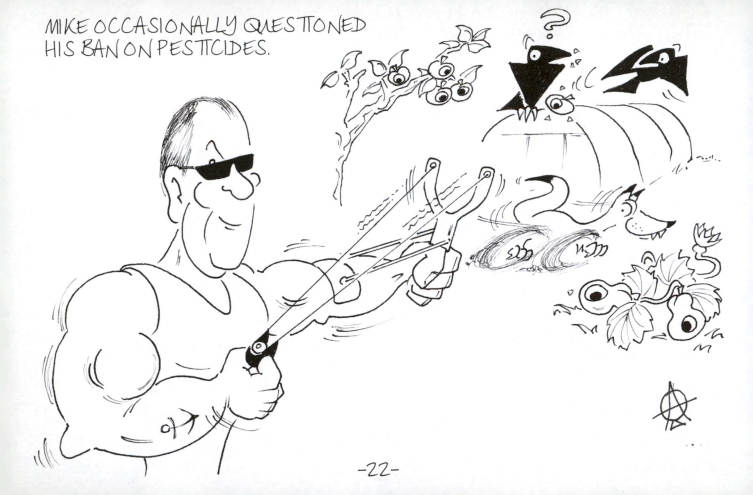

YOU MIGHT WANT THIS NEXT TIME YOU TRY PLANTING BY THE MOON.

MIKE BEGAN TO THINK HIS BARGAIN SHED FROM FREECYLE WAS A MISTAKE.

Foodie Matters

BEING THRIFTY, FRED SAW NOTHING WRONG WITH
HIS CHOICE OF CHRISTMAS CRACKERS...

THE VILLAGE STORE CLEARLY DIDN'T SUPPORT THE BARTER ECONOMY.

THE BREAKFAST TABLE DILEMMA – ONE EGG OR TWO?

IT'S A BAKING COMPETITION WITH THE W.I., NOT WITH THE WII.

SHE WAS QUITE PLEASED WITH HER FIRST ATTEMPT AT HOME MADE SAUSAGES.

WHAT'S THIS? I ASKED IF I COULD HAVE SOME BATTERY CHICKENS.

WHAT GREAT SERVICE, BEING CARRIED TO YOUR TABLE.

DEARLY BELOVED, WE ARE GATHERED HERE TODAY TO MAKE OUR DAILY BREAD...AND CHEESE...AND SAUSAGES...

-43-

All Sorts of Eco Stuff

OH SHOOT, I THINK I'VE TRODDEN IN A CARBON FOOTPRINT.

HONEST, IT'S A SPITTING COBRA.

BEAT THE HOSEPIPE BAN....IDEA No 7

"...AND THEY PLOUGH THROUGH ANYTHING."

THE SALESMAN WAS GOOD, BUT FARMER TAN DECIDED A
NEW CHELSEA TRACTOR WAS NOT FOR HIM.

THE SOLUTION TO GREENHOUSE GASES WAS NOW OBVIOUS.....

....NO MORE BAKED BEANS ON TOAST FOR BREAKFAST.

THEY ARRIVED IN THE VILLAGE CLAIMING TO BE FROM THE WATER CONSERVATION SOCIETY.

THE MET OFFICE SAID TO EXPECT A HEAVY DROP OF RAIN TODAY.

A Field of Cows

LOOK, BEEF DRIPPING.

MILK IN YOUR TEA DEAR...BOTTLED OR DRAUGHT?

EXCUSE ME BUT HAVEN'T I SEEN YOU ON TELEVISION?

DAISY WOULD MILK ANY PHOTO OPPORTUNITY.

Wildlife

HE WANTED A HEDGE, SAID IT WOULD ENCOURAGE WILDLIFE...

HE WENT TO A BEER FEST WITH GEORGE YESTERDAY AND I
HAVEN'T SEEN HIM SINCE.

WHAT'S GOING ON? OUR FAVOURITE EATERY HAS BEEN FENCED OFF.

HOMBRES, HEET LOOK LIKE HONLY 2 OF US CAN GO ON.

THE ROOMS YOU BOOKED, WERE THEY BOTH ON SWEETS?

WELCOME TO THE COUNTRY. CLEAN AIR, BEAUTIFUL SCENERY, PICTURESQUE VILLAGES, FRESH PRODUCE...NO BULL.

Red Tape

ZEB AND ZEE FELT THEIR PICNIC HAD
BEEN SPOILT.

MA O'FLAHERTY HAD STILL NOT CONVINCED THE LAW THAT HER
POTATO RECYCLING BUSINESS WAS LEGITIMATE.

ZEB AND ZEE ADMITTED GROWING THEIR OWN, BUT INSISTED THE TOMATOES WERE FOR PERSONAL USE ONLY.

SINCE NOVEMBER 2004, VARIOUS LAWS MAKE IT ILLEGAL FOR DOGS TO CHASE MICE, HARES, DEER, FOXES AND SQUIRRELS...

...BUT NOT RATS AND RABBITS.

NO, IT'S LIGHTLY SAUTEED IN BUTTER WITH GARLIC AND HERBS, DEFINITELY NOT POACHED.

Sheep Hurdles

ZEB AND ZEE HAD FOUND THE PERFECT DOG. IT WAS A CLEAR
CASE OF COLLIE FLOWER POWER.

HE'S ALWAYS HERE. IT'S THE DAILY LLAMA.

MORNING MONEY HENNY. THE NAMES KEN, CHICK...KEN.

IT BECAME QUITE CLEAR THAT THEY DIDN'T LIKE THEIR NEW ARK.

RESIST THE TEMPTATION, CHRISTMAS IS COMING.

SORRY. NO NOAH HERE AND THIS IS CHICKENS ONLY.

NO, HE'S STUDYING FOR HIS ENGLISH LITERATURE EXAM. I THINK IT'S THE TALE OF THE COCK AND FOX BY CHICKEN CHAUCER.

I CAN'T BELIEVE YOU JUST SIT THERE WATCHING CORONATION CHICKEN AND EASTHENDERS.

DO YOU STILL THINK I LOOK OLD?

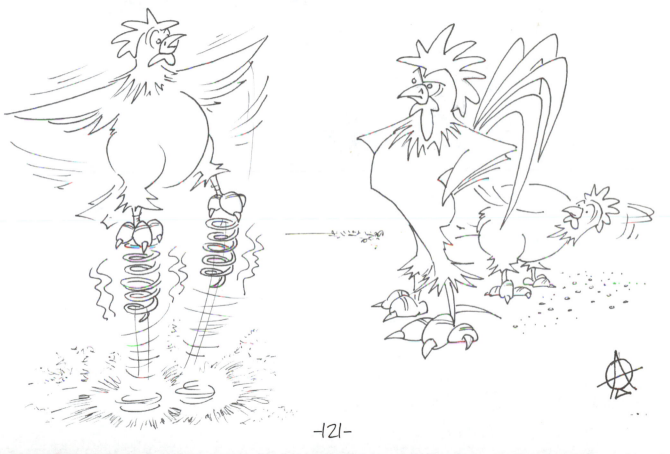

I started drawing seriously at boarding school. I was never really interested in painting still life stuff so I drew caricatures of the teaching staff, more for the amusement of my friends, probably not the staff!

On leaving school I moved to Germany initially and then to West Berlin. I worked as a grounds maintenance supervisor but also freelanced drawing cartoons for a local newspaper. When I left Germany my options were career or art college to do a degree in graphic design.

So I came back to the UK and embarked on what was a successful career for nearly 20 years.

In my spare time though, I received commissions for cartoons, posters, caricatures, training literature illustration and designs.

Eventually the internal politics and overbearing beaurocracy caused me to radically rethink my life and to look for an exit strategy from the rat race.

After gaining horticultural qualifcations with the RHS I resigned from my secure, well paid job with its very attractive pension.

My wife, Nadine, and I set up our own gardening business 4 years ago in pursuit of a better quality of life which we feel we have achieved.

Garden design work and subscribing to Home Farmer magazine inspired me to start cartooning again.

I have 2 great children, Ben and Abi, also 2 dogs and 2 chickens.

Les Ellis (lesquasiart@aol.com)

Any Fool Can Be a.....Middle Aged Downshifter
By Mike Woolnough
with cartoons by Les Ellis

Mike and Sue Woolnough's quest for the good life is beset with frustration, but also with anecdotes and whimsy as that elusive holy grail of self-sufficiency is pursued, approached and cornered but ultimately never quite attained. It is an ongoing battle with nature in the form of goats with attitude, the paramility wing of squirreldom, crows from hell and man in the form of beaurocracy and other disappointments and setbacks!

With a well balanced mix of realism, occasional pathos and a sense of humour ranging from the good natured to the gallows variety, Mike recounts with great candour his journey from furniture retailer to self-sufficient good lifer.

ISBN 9781904871576

The Chicken Lover's Cartoon Book

with cartoons by Arnold Wiles

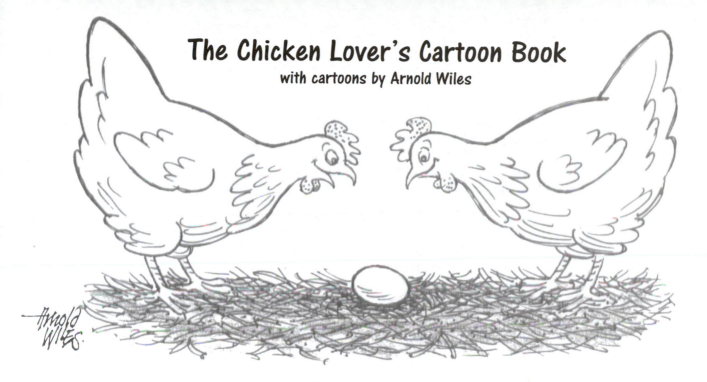

"Cute at that age, aren't they?"

60 specially commissioned cartoons by celebrated countryside cartoonist Arnold Wiles.
ISBN 9781904871996

The Good Life Press Ltd. publishes a wide range of titles for the smallholder, 'goodlifer' and farmer. We also publish **Home Farmer,** the monthly magazine for anyone who wants to grab a slice of the good life - whether they live in the country or the city. Other titles of interest include:

A Guide to Traditional Pig Keeping by Carol Harris
Any Fool Can Be a....Middle Aged Downshifter by Mike Woolnough
Build It!....With Pallets by Joe Jacobs
Craft Cider Making by Andrew Lea
Making Country Wines, Ales and Cordials by Brian Tucker
Making Jams and Preserves by Diana Sutton
No Time To Grow by Tim Wootton
Raising Chickens by Mike Woolnough
Raising Goats by Felicity Stockwell
The Frugal Life by Piper Terrett
The Medicine Garden by Rachel Corby
The Sausage Book by Paul Peacock
The Sheep Book for Smallholders by Tim Tyne
The Smoking and Curing Book by Paul Peacock
Worms and Wormeries by Mike Woolnough
and plenty more.....

www.goodlifepress.co.uk
www.homefarmer.co.uk